HEALING OUR

ANGER

SEVEN WAYS TO MAKE
PEACE IN A HOSTILE WORLD

HEALING OUR

ANGER

SEVEN WAYS TO MAKE
PEACE IN A HOSTILE WORLD

Dr. MICHAEL OBSATZ

Augsburg

MINNEAPOLIS

HEALING OUR ANGER
Seven Ways to Make Peace in a Hostile World

Scripture quotations are from the New Revised Standard Version Bible, copyright © 1989 by the Division of Christian Education of the National Council of the Churches of Christ in the U.S.A. and are used by permission.

Excerpted material by David Decker appearing on page 5 is adapted from "Controlling Anger—Before it Controls You," copyright © 1992 American Psychological Association. Reprinted (or adapted) with permission.

Excerpted material by Gail Sheehy on page 42 is from *Understanding Men's Passages* (1998), and is copyright © Random House. Used by permission.

Cited material by Sidney Simon is from *Forgiveness,* and copyright © 1990 Dr. Sidney B. Simon and Suzanne Simon. Used by permission of Warner Books, Inc.

Brief quotations and excerpted material by Lewis B. Smedes are from *Shame and Grace* by Lewis B. Smedes, copyright © 1993 Lewis B. Smedes. Reprinted by permission of HarperCollins Publishers, Inc.

Cited material from *The Anger Workbook* by Les Carter, Frank Minirth, and Paul Meier is copyright © 1993 Thomas Nelson Publishers. Used by permission.

Cover photograph copyright © 2000 PhotoDisc. Used by permission.
Cover design by Timothy W. Larson
Book design by Ann Rehfeldt

Library of Congress Cataloging-in-Publication Data

Obsatz, Michael.
    Healing our anger: seven ways to make peace in a hostile world / Michael Obsatz.
      p. cm.
    Includes bibliographical references.
    ISBN 0-8066-3890-7 (alk. paper)
1. Anger 2. Anger—Case studies. I. Title.

BF575.A5 O27 2000
152.4'7—dc21
                                        99-053601

Manufactured in the U.S.A.   AF 9-3890

04   03   02   01   00   2   3   4   5   6   7   8   9   10

To my three children,
Sharyn, Kevin, and Molly

~

CONTENTS

INTRODUCTION

WHO SAYS ANGER IS A PROBLEM?

We do know that we must do more to reach out to our children and teach them to express their anger and to resolve their conflicts with words, not weapons.

— President William Jefferson Clinton, in response to the Columbine High School massacre

On April 20, 1999, two adolescent boys described as angry outcasts attacked fellow students with guns and explosives in Littleton, Colorado. Twenty-three people were hospitalized, and twelve students and one teacher were killed before the gunmen, Eric Harris, 18, and Dylan Klebold, 17, killed themselves. Eric and Dylan had been teased and ostracized by fellow students. For more than a year, they plotted to bomb their school as a way to retaliate for the way they were treated. Eric's and Dylan's anger built up and finally exploded in tragedy.

In horror, millions of Americans came to learn of the extent of the boys' anger as stories and footage of the massacre were released to the public. Many were shocked by the events at Littleton. They wondered how young boys could be that angry. U.S. Attorney General Janet Reno flew to Denver and expressed concern about American youth not being able to control their anger and channel it productively.

Prior to Littleton, Americans experienced the eruption of explosive anger from adolescents Kip Kinkel, Michael Carneal, Luke Woodham, Mitchell Johnson, and Andrew Golden. These youth killed fifteen people and wounded forty-four others. Since Littleton, a high school student named T. J. Solomon wounded several of his classmates in Conyers, Georgia.

1

These horrific cases point to a lack of understanding about the sources and significance of anger. Hurt and rejection can turn to anger and outrage. Outrage may result in violence and destruction. In some cases, those who are hurt and angry turn their weapons on themselves. In the case of the Littleton tragedy, Eric and Dylan seemed to be on a suicide mission.

This book is about anger and the different ways we handle it. A serious mental health problem in the United States, the buildup of anger can destroy not only the angry, but others as well. Thousands die yearly due to violent eruptions of anger.

We all have moments of hurt, rejection, and outrage. Are you having problems with your anger? Are there times when you blow up over minor things and feel bad about it later? And what about other people's anger? Do you find yourself unsure of how to deal with an angry adolescent, an angry partner, or an angry coworker or boss?

As a society, we seem to be angrier than we have ever been. People are stressed at work, on the highways, and at home. Domestic violence affects couples of all races, ages, and classes. Some people are court ordered to take anger management classes. More people are being injured or killed on our roadways and in the workplace due to road rage and office violence.

Are you like me? Sometimes I am so stressed that the slightest disappointment or inconvenience can result in an angry outburst. My sense of injustice leads to anger. My impatience leads to anger. My perfectionism leads to anger. My need to control leads to anger.

Anger can be destructive and, as we are witnessing, it can kill. But anger can also be a signal that we need to act, to evaluate something, to change something. Sometimes my anger has produced positive results. It has served as a motivator. It has helped me feel alive and vital. Sometimes, my anger has acted as a wake-up call—for instance, perhaps I needed to confront someone who was treating me disrespectfully. My anger has also represented a sign of vulnerability and has led to greater intimacy with others. All of these are things that David Decker points out in his article "Anger: Your Enemy or Your Ally." When recognized and used properly, our anger can result in positive changes: new laws, social changes, a healthier state of morality.

The goal of this book is to help you develop your personal power, a healthy support system, a strong faith in God's grace, and a meaningful sense of purpose, so the little annoyances of life no longer cripple you with anger. Many of the chapters offer suggestions and exercises to put some of those chapter's messages into practice. Each of the letters of H-E-A-L-I-N-G begins a chapter that moves you along the path.

This book examines both the positive and negative effects of our anger and looks at anger from physical, emotional, social, and spiritual perspectives. Examples, rewritten for confidentiality, from my work with families and individuals are included to provide context. You will have an opportunity to take a quiz to discover your Anger Quotient (AQ). You will also learn short-term and long-term ways of dealing with and healing your anger, and you will explore strategies for coping with the anger of others—strategies for saving yourself pain and frustration.

Chapter 1, "How Does Our Anger Work," describes the anatomy and complexity of anger. We begin to understand what anger looks like by answering the following questions: Are we an angry society? What does anger look like? What are the different types of anger? Is there a positive use for anger? Why are many of us so angry? Why are some people angrier than others? Where did we learn our anger responses? What does our anger do to us physically, socially, and emotionally?

Chapter 2, "Effectively Handling Your Own Anger," suggests concrete ways to calm down, including detachment, introspection, and time-outs. This chapter also offers ways of using words to bring calm and become peaceful.

Chapter 3, "Avoiding Hostile Confrontations," examines how to cope with other people's anger. Various settings are explored, including anger in the workplace, anger in the family, and anger on the highways.

Chapter 4, "Learning to Destress Yourself," focuses on relaxation techniques, finding peaceful role models, developing a healthy support network, and finding trustworthy helpers for medical, legal, dental, and other types of maintenance.

Chapter 5, "Instilling in Yourself Realistic Attitudes Toward Life," helps you examine your expectations. In this chapter, you learn how to let go, grieve losses and disappointments, and develop a forgiving attitude toward yourself, others, and life itself.

Chapter 6, "Nourishing Yourself through Spiritual Resources," focuses on biblical messages about God's grace and the importance of humility, generosity, compassion, and trust. This chapter also helps you develop a strong sense of purpose, leading to spiritual and emotional empowerment.

Chapter 7, "Giving Anger a Positive Outlet," encourages you to respond to your anger with constructive action.

As you read through the seven chapters, I hope you will find yourself both empowered and relieved, perhaps even transformed: your anger turned to understanding, your fear turned to love, and your feelings of powerlessness and frustration turned to a sense of personal empowerment. In reading this book, you may find that you no longer need to be perfect, that you can slow down and still achieve your goals. The world, with its limits and mistakes, is still lovable and joyful. And God is always present to help you cope with difficult and challenging situations.

May your reading of this book help you develop a sense of purpose and an attitude of forgiveness, both of which can encourage and equip you to live joyfully and peacefully in an imperfect, and sometimes hostile, world.

1

HOW DOES OUR ANGER WORK?

Anger begins as a physical experience. All strong emotions—anger, fear, surprise, and excitement—trigger powerful hormones that are released into the body. This is the automatic "fight or flight" as a "warning signal" that lets you know when something is going on around you that needs to be attended to. Anger can also serve as an energizer and a catalyst that helps to motivate you. Anger can also allow you to become vulnerable and thus open the door to intimacy.

— David Decker, "Anger: Your Enemy or Your Ally"

Are We an Angry Society?

IT IS IMPOSSIBLE TO SAY IF AMERICAN SOCIETY is angrier than other societies or angrier than it has been in the past. But it seems to be so, perhaps because, with the ever-present media, we are more aware of people's anger. In this chapter, we will look at some of the possible causes of anger in this country and some ways in which that anger manifests itself.

1. *People seem to experience more stress and pressure than before.*
   People have many demands on their time, which means they are left to perform several tasks at once. Many Americans hold more than one job. In most two-parent families, for example, parents must manage their careers, housework, and child rearing. The responsibilities and related stress for single parents can be even greater.

   The Johnson family provides one example of the stress and pressure many Americans face. Bonnie and Terry are the parents of

Eric, 4, and Sandra, 2. Bonnie works part-time as a receptionist. Terry manages a local printing shop. He also works some evenings delivering local newspapers. Between them, Terry and Bonnie work seventy hours a week. They are putting money away for their children's education, but they rarely see each other or have meals together.

2. *Americans are more diverse than ever.*
We have all types of people from many different cultures living within close quarters, and unfortunately not everyone works to understand and communicate within this diversity. Thus, for some, getting along with people who have different cultures, values, and habits takes extra energy and may cause stress. Crowding can result in friction and the need to fight for space and privacy.

3. *Information and technology overload affect everyone.*
We have more information to process and more technology to learn about than previous generations did. As a computer-reliant society, we are more dependent upon technology and less reliant upon each other. As a result, we often don't practice, or learn, some of the skills needed for human interaction. We isolate ourselves, spending much of our time plugged into computers, CD players, video games, and televisions.

Twelve-year-old Charlie is a good example of the isolation made possible by technology. He has a CD player, TV, computer, and video games in his room. His mother, Nancy, says he spends hours in his room, sometimes not even joining the family for dinner. She worries that Charlie is not learning social skills and is not spending more time with his friends.

4. *Some people sense an erosion of trust in authority figures.*
Aware of misuse of power by some in authority, we may see our trust of politicians, clergy, police, teachers, and others erode. Some people may feel angry that they cannot trust more people in power.

5. *Geographic mobility can make people feel isolated and lost.*
Geographic mobility often separates people from the support networks of family and close friends. As we experience greater distance

from those we love, we find ourselves trying to make new friends and build new support networks. This takes time, energy, and work—and doesn't always guarantee success. Anger can come from feeling isolated and lost.

The Brokowsky family, for example, has moved six times in the last nine years. Their closest relative is 800 miles away. Since Marjorie Brokowsky believes they will move again in the next two years, she hesitates to invest much time in her neighborhood. She claims it makes it painful to leave if she cares too much about those who live next door.

6. *We live in an era seemingly preoccupied with instant gratification.*
A preoccupation with instant gratification can manifest itself in self-centeredness or a sense of entitlement. When life does not gratify instantly or meet expectations, frustration and anger can result. Self-centered people have difficulty seeing life from other points of view, which can lead to a "my-way-or-the-highway" mentality. This lack of patience, tolerance, and understanding of others' rights can manifest itself as anger. Road rage is an example of this self-centered thinking. Drivers who experience road rage seem to expect to have the road to themselves.

Pat Sagara is worried that since her family came to the United States from Japan, her two children have learned to be too material, too self-centered, too set on instant gratification. She refuses to indulge them by buying them everything they want. Instead, she gives them one trendy item of their choice each year.

7. *Complicated family relationships can cause stress and anger.*
Many children and adults live in blended families. There are step-grandparents, stepparents, and stepchildren. According to George Dickinson, more than 25 percent of all children born in the United States in the early 1980s will have more than two parents. Some children claim that they are sharing space with virtual strangers. With a relatively high divorce rate, there are angry legal disputes, custody battles, and broken dreams. Many stepfamilies are born out of loss, and anger is one of the stages of grieving those losses.

The Rydell-Smith family works hard to make life as a stepfamily smooth and happy. Johnny leaves to visit his dad every other weekend. Kathy comes to visit her dad once a month. The number of family members at home is continually changing from three to five people. Even well-planned schedules can become stressful at times. This adds to the general stresses experienced in all families.

8. *Single-parent families may experience more poverty and stress.*
Single-parent families are more likely to know poverty and stress than two-parent families. United States government statistics report that in 1988, 43 percent of elementary-age children in single-parent families lived below the poverty line. Living in poverty, where basic necessities such as food, space, and security are scarce, can lead to feelings of inadequacy, powerlessness, frustration, and anger.

Melanie is a single parent. Her sources of stress are common to many single-parent families. She is trying to feed five children on the limited salary she earns working as a maid. She is going deeper into debt, struggling to pay for her small apartment, food, clothing, and bills. In addition to these stressors, her children are starting to hang out with others outside the house. She is worried about them, especially her son Tyrell, getting caught up in gang activity. Some gang members promised Tyrell a new bike if he joined their gang.

9. *Political correctness can lead to frustrations.*
While the benefits of political correctness are many—awareness of and empathy with the needs, values, and beliefs of those who are different from ourselves, for example—it does hold its own sources of frustration. One such frustration is the seeming pressure to conform. Some people feel angry when they believe they are forced to do so.

Chris, a student at a small liberal arts college, is experiencing criticism for his conservative political views. Chris believes that it is more politically correct at his college to be liberal. Yet Chris is conservative and is experiencing growing frustration and anger because his views are often criticized by others. For Chris, those criticizing him appear to be intolerant of his beliefs and eager to force him to conform to theirs.

10. *Undisciplined venting can produce destructive anger.*
    The "let it all hang out" philosophy of the last thirty years has encouraged undisciplined venting as a way of relieving stress. Many people believe that expressing outrage will automatically dissipate it. Recent studies have shown, however, that undisciplined, unconstructive venting of anger does not necessarily reduce it or associated hostility. Brad Bushman and psychologists from Iowa State University and Case Western Reserve reported in the *Journal of Personality and Social Psychology* (January 1999) that hitting a punching bag only increased the amount of anger participants felt. Seven hundred college students were more hostile to their partners after having an opportunity to "let off stream" by punching a bag.

11. *Many people lack appropriate communication skills.*
    Many people lack the appropriate communication skills necessary to express and cope with their feelings. The problem is further complicated by the fact that the communication skills we teach our children are often different for boys and girls. Boys are commonly socialized to vent anger but to hide more vulnerable feelings (for instance, sadness and fear). Girls, conversely, often learn to repress their anger. Thus we often find ourselves faced with different, but inadequate approaches to anger and situations that produce it.

    When Jon, age nine, was feeling sad and hurt, for example, he tended to express those feelings indirectly by exploding at his younger brother, Will. Once Jon's father, Gene, realized the reasons for Jon's venting against his brother, he was able to constructively reduce the outbursts by encouraging Jon to express his sad and vulnerable feelings in more positive ways.

12. *Litigious approaches to problem solving can encourage the use of anger.*
    Litigious solutions—with their expressions of anger and conflict—rather than discussion, mediation, and compromise, seem to have become the model for settling problems and conflicts.

13. *Our culture often encourages unrealistic pictures of life.*
    The culture around us often paints and upholds unrealistic pictures of life, success, and happiness. We sometimes dream up unrealistic

expectations as well. Some people, using these faulty measures, become depressed about their own lives, wishing for the easier and happier lives they see portrayed in the media and held up as ideals by their peers. Many are disappointed and frustrated when they go on diets and don't lose weight, or when they do lose weight and find their life is not noticeably different than before, or when they buy designer clothing or new cars but don't feel better about themselves.

Mark and Melissa had high expectations of their life together when they got married, but they soon discovered that their marriage did not match their expectations. After working with a counselor for six sessions, Mark and Melissa made some strides but needed to adjust their expectations of each other to be more realistic. They learned a lot about the work and effort a good marriage requires—work and effort that are a stark contrast to the happily-ever-after endings in the movies.

14. *The gap has widened between the rich and the poor.*
There are more people living in poverty than in previous years. Many people, including families, who live in poverty are also homeless. While poor people are not necessarily angrier than those who are wealthy, they can experience the anger and frustration that result from lacking basic necessities. Also, when people believe they lead undervalued lives with little hope, they may see little reason to curb their anger to prevent taking unnecessary risks.

Antonio has lived in poverty all his life and has no job. He thinks the world around him considers him inconsequential. Three of his friends have been killed, and he expects that he is next. There is no point, he claims, to taking care of himself or being nice to other people. So he has an I-don't-care attitude that expresses itself in explosive rage when he is angry.

15. *Many are searching for some sort of spiritual expression or connection.*
Those who experience spiritual disconnectedness may lack empathy and the capacity to forgive. They may experience life as painful or unsatisfying. Significantly, researchers suggest that some spiritual people are less angry than others. Their spiritual connectedness (and this does not necessarily mean participation in organized religion)

provides a foundation for compassion, empathy, and forgiveness. As discussed in chapter 5, Virginia psychologist Everett Worthington, director of the Templeton Foundation Campaign for Forgiveness Research, claims that forgiveness has the power to dissipate anger, mend marriages, and banish depression.

What Are Different Ways of Expressing Anger?

We all experience anger. Many of us are affected by some of the previously mentioned causes and manifestations of anger. While anger is a common human feeling, we have different thresholds for those things that cause it. Some of us get angry quickly and easily. Others are slower to feel anger. The American Psychological Association (APA) tells us that people use both conscious and unconscious processes in coping with angry feelings. Three approaches to anger are expressing, suppressing, and calming.

Expressing angry feelings in an assertive—not aggressive—manner is the healthiest way to handle them. To accomplish this, you state your needs clearly and firmly. Being assertive doesn't mean being pushy or demanding. When someone cuts ahead of me in line, I can firmly tell that person that I have waited for my position in line and don't believe it is fair to be pushed back any further.

Anger can be suppressed, and then converted. Anger turned inward can cause hypertension, high blood pressure, or depression, according to the APA. Passive-aggressive expressions of anger are indirect and can come out as sarcasm, cynicism, joking, teasing, perpetual lateness, or depression. My friend John has made sarcastic comments when he feels pushed around. These demonstrate to me that he is actually angry but not stating so directly.

Another process for coping with anger is to calm oneself. This involves recognition and acceptance of the feeling of anger, controlling internal responses, thinking of something peaceful, lowering your heart rate, and using verbal or visual methods to calm yourself down. When driving behind a particularly careless or slow driver, I can often feel myself becoming tense and angry. When I tell myself to be patient, slow down, and relax, I usually can feel myself unwind and become calmer.

What Are the Eight Types of Anger?

In addition to different ways of expressing anger, there are different types of anger. These types of anger may actually look different. Some of us may be more prone to one type than another. We may, however, have experienced all of these at one time or another.

1. *Chronic anger is an ongoing feeling of resentment toward others.*
   People who experience oppression may exhibit chronic anger. An example of a chronically angry person is one who tends to be hostile and negative no matter what situation he is in.

2. *Volatile anger comes and goes.*
   It is explosive, builds to rage, and expresses itself through verbal or physical aggression. An example of volatile anger can be found in a person who is kind some of the time but at other unpredictable times explodes with rage and aggression.

3. *Judgmental anger comes across in hypercritical statements.*
   A person who is judgmentally angry may appear to feel superior to others by belittling, shaming, or ridiculing them. In fact, many people who express judgmental anger may actually feel inferior to others. They often use judgmental anger to hide or repress their feelings of inferiority.

4. *Passive anger is suppressed anger that expresses itself indirectly.*
   The passively angry person has converted her anger into an alternative expression of it, such as being habitually late. A passively angry person may also withhold affection or love as a way of expressing anger.

5. *Overwhelmed anger arises when people believe they cannot handle the complexity of their life circumstances.*
   They are at a loss for coping with difficult situations, changes, or disappointments. They may lash out as a way of relieving pain, confusion, and tension.

6. *Retaliatory anger is specifically directed at another person or persons.*
   The angry individual directs retaliatory anger at the person or

persons whom he believes mistreated or hurt him. The person experiencing retaliatory anger does not feel that he has any other means for addressing perceived injustice.

7. ***Self-inflicted anger*** *is directed at ourselves.*
   When our anger becomes directed at ourselves, we may do detrimental things to ourselves. Self-inflicted anger can include negative self-talk, starvation, eating or drinking to excess, cutting oneself, and suicide.

8. ***Constructive anger*** *is anger we put to positive use.*
   If, out of our anger at injustice, we picket or march in protest, we may be attempting to create some type of positive change. Or, if we are angry at our parents for what we believed to be poor parenting we received as children, we may channel that anger into using healthier and more positive parenting techniques with our own children.

These types of anger can exist in the same person or in several people within the same family. Sometimes one family member's anger can trigger another family member's anger. Here is a brief case study of a family that shows how the individuals interact and how different types of anger are manifested in one family.

Maddie believes she was neglected as a child. She thinks her parents, Tom and Lois, paid more attention to her brother, Frank. They bragged about his sports successes and his good report cards. Frank went off to a good private college and then law school. He became one of the most respected lawyers in his community. After Maddie finished high school, she married Ken, who drives a delivery truck. Maddie works as a bookkeeper for a local restaurant. She earns minimum wage.

Frank married Jessica, who comes from a wealthy family. Jessica's parents ran their own business and were never home when Jessica was a child. Frank and Jessica now live in a large country-style home in the suburbs. Frank and Jessica have invited Maddie and Ken for dinner several times. Maddie goes reluctantly. She believes that Jessica doesn't like her and thinks Jessica tries to show her up with fine china and elegant meals. Ken tells Maddie that Jessica and Frank are just being good family to them.

Maddie is angry with Frank and Jessica. She is frustrated by what they have and by what she does not have. But the core of this anger is *chronic anger* at her parents. She is angry that they did not give her the same opportunity to attend college as they gave Frank. She is bitter because she feels she was not offered the chance to gain the skills necessary to have a more prestigious career and earn more money.

When Jessica talks about a social or charitable event she has sponsored, Maddie glances at Ken. It is a judgmental look. She is critical of Jessica's life, especially the fact that Jessica does not have to work outside the home. The family has plenty of discretionary money that they can give to charity. Maddie's *judgmental anger* seems to be directed more at Jessica than at Frank. It comes out in clipped words and sarcasm.

Ken has a drinking problem. When he drinks too much, he has been known to lash out at anyone in sight, usually Maddie or the children (Rob, age thirteen, and Sarah, age eleven). When things don't go his way, Ken can feel his breath shorten, his body tense, and his voice become louder. He explodes in *volatile anger* and sometimes smashes a dish or vase on the floor. After this explosion, he is remorseful and quiet and attempts to apologize. The quiet time lasts for a while until Ken is upset again.

Ken's explosions frighten the children. Rob has become quiet lately and spends most of his time in his room. He is furious at his father for losing his temper and expresses this through *passive anger.* He doesn't do his chores. He refuses to go hunting with his father on the weekends. He avoids him at mealtimes by eating early or late and microwaving his own dinners.

Sarah responds to this situation by trying to starve herself. At eleven, she weighs only fifty-nine pounds. Her *self-inflicted anger* comes out in an eating disorder. Neither of her parents knows about her purging after meals. Sarah also hurts herself by putting herself down in front of her friends. Her grades have suffered as she does not do her homework or study for her tests.

Maddie has decided not to have contact with her mother, Lois, because she believes her parents set her up for a miserable life. Lois lives two hours away. Maddie's father died three years ago. She has not called her mother in months and doesn't visit her on holidays. She has not sent her mother a card for Mother's Day in six years. Maddie's *retaliatory anger* is her attempt to even the score, to get back at her mother for what she believes to be parenting mistakes.

Lois is now seventy and in poor health. She has a small income from her husband's pension but has difficulty taking care of her house. The laundry piles up, the dishes stay dirty, and the yard is overgrown. She has few friends and is having difficulty driving. There are times when Lois goes into a rage because her life seems so unmanageable and out of control. Her *overwhelmed anger* comes out in a variety of ways—yelling, screaming, crying, and temper tantrums.

Jessica also experiences her own anger. She is angry at her parents for being gone all the time when she was a child. But she has turned her anger into a positive effort to be a better parent to her son, Lee. Jessica's *constructive use of anger* is different than the rest of her family's ways of handling anger.

What Does Anger Do to Us?

Consequences of Unhealthy Anger

In the case study above, each of these family members demonstrates a different type of anger. Jessica attempts to deal with her anger in a healthy, constructive manner. The other family members clearly do not deal with their anger in healthy ways. And, like them, if we do not deal with our anger in healthy ways, we risk certain consequences.

1. *The Health Risks of Anger*
   Some ways of expressing anger may actually have a negative impact upon us physically. When we react in anger, we are doing so because a fight-or-flight response has been triggered. Our anger is a natural response to frustration, violation, hurt, or loss. Our anger can definitely produce bodily symptoms, according to Carol Tavris, author of *Anger*. Some bodily symptoms may include blushing, sweating, numbness, chills, shuddering, prickly sensations, the grinding of teeth, the clenching of fists, scowling, dry throat, hoarseness, stomach pains, quickened heart rate, palpitations, and breathlessness. When we are angry, some of us might experience insomnia, nightmares, or other sleep disturbances. Some might overeat. Others may have difficulty eating, swallowing, or eliminating.

Some research studies have shown that excessive anger can be a factor in heart disease. Other studies show that intense anger can cause ulcers, colitis, and high blood pressure. Still others report that hostile people are at greater risk for having heart attacks.

2. *Social Consequences of Anger*
Excessive anger and hostility can lead to higher levels of stress and social isolation. Overtly angry people tend to push other people away. People often shy away from excessively angry and hostile people. People become fearful that such a person will erupt into a rage at a moment's notice, and they don't want to be around when that happens. When angry people become isolated, they can be prone to more anger.

3. *Brain Functions: Memory and Speech*
Anger can affect our memory. When very angry, we may forget things or even black out. Anger affects brain functioning by inhibiting clear thinking and problem solving. Anger can get in the way of coherent speech patterns. We may jumble our words. Keith Sehnert, author of *Dr. Sehnert's New Guide to Managing Your Stress,* says that if we lose control while we are angry, we might experience "brain fog."

4. *Anger and Accidents*
Physiological effects of anger can cause a person to be accident-prone. When obsessed with anger, some people ignore necessary precautions, drive recklessly, or refuse to wear seat belts. People in the midst of expressing excessive anger may take unnecessary risks and don't always care about protecting their lives and the lives of others.

5. *Anger and Low Self-Esteem*
Excessively angry people tend to alienate others. As a result, they may suffer low self-esteem. They may have to continually find new people to boost their esteem. Feelings of abandonment and loneliness can add to their low self-esteem.

6. *Anger and Job Loss*
People who are quick to anger and lose their temper easily may have difficulty keeping their jobs. If they are considered unable to

handle stress or deal effectively with coworkers or clients, they may be terminated. Hostile responses to bosses often lead to negative consequences.

7. *Anger and Marital Problems*
Couples who experience repeated conflict, fighting, and hostility often break up. Domestic violence in marriage is often related to a spouse's uncontrolled anger and his or her inability to control impulses to strike out. People who can't control their anger or who express it in volatile or violent ways have a difficult time staying in long-term, committed relationships. Excessive anger is one of the major sources of conflict and stress in the relationships of couples who have come to see me for counseling.

8. *Anger, Depression, and Suicide*
People who bottle up their anger and do not find ways to calm down and express it in peaceful ways may end up feeling depressed, sometimes suicidal. Because anger is often a cry for help, understanding, or support, people who continually suppress their anger and don't ask for what they need can end up in severe emotional pain.

9. *Anger's Effects on Children*
Children who grow up in families where anger is expressed disrespectfully often lack valuable interpersonal skills. If they witness domestic violence, they may grow up fearful of relationships and unable to sustain them. Children watching parents express only anger may not learn how to share feelings of joy, sadness, disappointment, or fear.

10. *Anger in Our Neighborhoods*
Anger and hostility in neighborhoods can make residents fear leaving their homes. They may believe they are not safe and might move to other neighborhoods.

11. *Anger and Violence in Our Schools*
In the past few years, we have read about numerous school shootings across the United States in which students vented their anger and retaliated against others. Some children fear going to school.

We are now using metal detectors, increased security, and alarm systems in our schools.

12. *National Hostility*

Angry responses from public figures help create a general negative attitude among our people. Political campaigns often include nasty attacks, angry responses, and harsh criticisms. Angry guests on television talk shows viewed by millions often demonstrate inappropriate and unhealthy ways of dealing with anger.

Positive Consequences of Anger

Anger can lead to constructive action. A number of mothers who lost loved ones in drunk driving accidents formed Mothers Against Drunk Driving (MADD) because they were angry—and because they wanted to use that anger to make a difference. They mobilized and worked to create stricter laws, and they increased the enforcement of laws that take away licenses of drivers who abuse alcohol and then drive. There are many other groups that formed as an angry response to some type of injustice. Anger can lead to positive action and social change.

Where Did We Learn to Express or Suppress Our Anger?

Now that we have examined the consequences of anger, we might wonder why some people have more problems with anger than other people do. Where did we learn to express our anger the way we do? Do we teach boys different messages about anger than girls?

Some textbooks about gender role socialization claim that boys are taught aggression, assertiveness, and anger as part of being male. Thus, boys might be more overt in expressing volatile anger or retaliatory anger. Girls, on the other hand, may be taught to suppress their anger and find more indirect and covert ways of expressing it. In groups, girls may redirect their anger by excluding someone or gossiping about them.

Deborah Tannen, author of *You Just Don't Understand,* discusses differences in male and female communication patterns. She believes that females want to maintain intimate relationships at all costs and may not express their anger or frustrations directly for fear of losing those relationships. Girls and women, according to Tannen, may be encouraged to be the peacemakers and placaters. While boys who express their anger through physical violence may be punished, girls who express passive anger or self-inflicted anger may not receive punishment.

There are several theories about the differences between males and females with respect to the expression and suppression of anger, but there are also many exceptions. Katie, an eleven-year-old, is just as vocal and expressive of her anger as her older brother, Tim, is of his. When Katie was younger, she was criticized by her parents for being openly angry. She told them she had every right to express her anger as directly as her brother.

Wayne, on the other hand, has always had trouble directly expressing anger. He is emotionally sensitive and, when upset, he cries rather than yells. Katie and Wayne are two of the many children who cross theoretical gender lines when it comes to anger expression.

Some theorists believe that we learn to express or suppress our anger in our family of origin. If we had a dad who was angry all the time, we learn it is acceptable to express anger. If we had a mom who expressed passive anger, we may adopt her style of anger redirection. Many children, however, grow up to act in the opposite manner of their parents. Tony watched his father, an alcoholic, explode in anger at his older brother for much of his childhood. As a result, Tony vowed to be more careful and reserved about expressing his anger. Angry parents may or may not produce angry children.

Some geneticists believe that there are brain differences between short-fused and longer-fused people. This brain research is still in the beginning phases, so nothing is conclusive about which parts of the brain might contribute to volatile anger expressions and which might contribute to greater anger control.

Some people may be more prone to express their anger because they have higher expectations of themselves and others. Sometimes these people are called Type A personalities. Wendy defines herself as a Type A personality because she is meticulous in her work, always prompt, and perfectly dressed. When things don't go her way, however, she is able to relax and take it in stride. In other words, not all Type A personalities are the same.

Some people believe that certain ethnic groups are more likely to express their anger. A stereotype of Italians says that they are more verbally expressive in general, making sweeping gestures and expressing all emotions more freely. A stereotype of Norwegians says that they are more stoic, patient, and self-effacing. However, I have seen and heard Norwegians explode in anger and Italians calmly and quietly express their frustrations and hurts.

What seems to matter most in the expression of anger is what happens when children actually reveal their anger. If a child is rewarded for outbursts of anger, that child will probably express anger more overtly. If a child is shamed for overtly expressing anger, that child may find other ways of expressing anger more indirectly.

None of the above categories—gender, family of origin, or ethnic background—clearly determine how publicly or privately we express our anger. We are all unique individuals, and we develop our anger expression (or suppression) style from many different types of stimuli.

It is clear, however, that anger can take its toll on all of us—physically, intellectually, emotionally, and socially—and that there are ways of calming ourselves down. Before we look at calming techniques, take a few minutes to assess your own anger quotient.

What Is Your Anger Quotient?

Answer the following questions with 3 points for "most of the time," 2 points for "sometimes," and 1 point for "rarely or never."

_____ 1. When I disagree with my coworkers, I tend to get angry.

_____ 2. I make judgmental and critical remarks about others.

_____ 3. I get very upset when my children misbehave.

_____ 4. My anger comes out as yelling or hitting.

_____ 5. I am very impatient when I have to wait.

_____ 6. I get angry at myself when I make a mistake.

_____ 7. When I read about or see the cruelty and injustice in the world, I become very angry.

_____ 8. I have very high expectations about life and myself.

_____ 9. I get angry at my wife, husband, or significant other.

_____ 10. I am very sensitive about what others think of me.

For the following questions, give yourself 1 point for "most of the time," 2 points for "sometimes," and 3 points for "rarely or never."

_____ 11. I know how to destress and relax when I feel tense.

_____ 12. I know why I'm doing what I'm doing.

_____ 13. I believe that God loves me and will take care of me.

_____ 14. I have supportive people whom I can call if I need help.

_____ 15. I forgive others who have hurt me.

_____ 16. I can let go of hurts, disappointments, and grudges.

_____ 17. I have compassion for others.

_____ 18. I am grateful for what I have.

_____ 19. I pray to God.

_____ 20. I believe God loves me even when I make mistakes.

Answer the following questions with a brief statement.

21. What are some ways you have found to relieve your stress?

22. What are the most common ways you express your anger?

23. Are there particular types of people who anger you?

24. What losses have you experienced lately?

25. How have you grieved those losses?

26. How much violence do you watch on television or in the movies?

27. What do you do so that you will grow spiritually closer to God?

28. What words do you tell yourself when you are having a hard day?

29. Do you tell your close friends and family members that you care about them?

30. What are some behaviors that cause you to become very angry?

Scoring for the first twenty questions

45–60 points:	You may be quick to anger.
30–44 points:	You may be occasionally quick to anger but also often cool-tempered
Below 30 points:	You may be generally calm and patient.

Whatever your anger quotient, you will find the next chapters useful. Having explored the hows and whys of anger and some possible implications, we will now look at ways to handle our own anger and to cope effectively with the anger of others around us.

2

EFFECTIVELY HANDLING YOUR OWN ANGER

When you are able to see anger coming—to detect it early on—you have a significantly greater opportunity to use it constructively. Because of your foresight you can prepare to resist habitual ways of expressing it, especially if those ways have proven destructive. You also have time to strategize about the most effective ways of using your anger to pursue personal and relational objectives.

— Neil Clark Warren, *Make Anger Your Ally*

WE ALL HAVE THOSE TIMES when we feel pushed over the edge. Anger builds up in us, and as much as we try to control it, it bursts forth, sometimes with yelling and screaming, sometimes with striking out. A variety of techniques can be used to handle anger. The first of these is to realize what causes your anger to build. There may be certain events that happen in a day to cause you to feel angry.

- Your car won't start.
- Your son leaves his bike in the driveway, and you almost hit it.
- There is a traffic jam on the freeway.
- Your boss is in an especially grumpy mood when he arrives in the morning.
- The breakfast you ordered does not arrive as you ordered it, and it is cold.
- Your assigned parking place at work is taken by someone else.
- A client you have to see is late, forcing you to move all of your appointments to a later time.

- Your daughter forgot to tell you what door she would be waiting at to be picked up after school soccer practice.
- You get home to find the dishwasher spewing water all over the kitchen floor.
- The mail contains a tax bill for a thousand dollars more than last year.

For many people, anger builds throughout a day, and they are not aware of it happening until they reach the boiling point. The explosion comes when a person has had just too many frustrations over a short period of time.

To avoid this, it is important to pay attention to each little thing that makes you angry and express your anger and frustration in some nonviolent way as the tension is building. Find a calm way of venting it before it piles up and becomes too big to release peacefully. One effective way of calming down is to breathe deeply, relax, and use calming words:

"This will all work out fine."
"I know I can handle this."
"I can slow myself down and relax."
"Nothing is so important that I need to get upset about it."
"I won't let this get the best of me."

Some people need a time-out, a breather. Take a short break. Go for a walk. Stretch yourself and breathe deeply. Read an inspiring quotation. Eat something that you really enjoy. All of these activities can take your mind off the build-up of tension that may be occurring.

Another technique you can use to manage your angry moments is to become aware of trigger words or events that cause your anger to build. You may be particularly sensitive to a look, a gesture, a situation, or a word that seems hurtful, undermining, or threatening. Write down a list of these triggers that may cause your frustration and your anger to build. Once you have your list, use some self-talk to disarm their power.

"I will not let slow drivers get to me."
"I will not let the word thoughtless make me angry."

Detachment is another way to cope with anger. If something happens that might make you very angry, try to step outside the situation and look upon it as an observer rather than as a person in the midst of it. Being detached and objective can help you not take things as personally. A detached way of looking at a potentially angering situation might be to tell yourself, "This situation is certainly odd. Here goes Joe again, trying to blame me for the mess he has gotten the company into. In the past, I think that would have infuriated me. Now, I see it as Joe's problem, not mine. He may try to make it my problem, but I will gently and directly let him know that I do not see it that way."

Another way to cope with your own anger build-up is to ask yourself, "Am I feeling any other emotion besides anger that anger might be masking? Am I actually hurt or sad or scared?" In order to do this, you have to calm down first, and then give yourself the time and space to look at your deeper feelings. Very often I get angry when I feel unappreciated or disrespected. At the bottom of my anger is hurt, and that pain is a reminder of times past when I was treated badly. While my anger seems to be about the current situation, much of it is about old baggage I am carrying around with me.

It may be helpful to explore that old baggage and understand past hurts and disappointments. You can do this through journaling, individual counseling, or becoming part of a support or therapy group. Keeping an anger journal, writing down just what makes you angry and why, can be a helpful way to get in touch with other feelings—hurt, sadness, fear, pain.

Many people become angry because they feel violated or abused. Again, it is helpful to detach from the situation enough to notice any way in which you feel your space, your privacy, your rights, or your feelings have been violated. By becoming more objective, you can begin to see patterns in your own behavior. When you notice patterns, you can make some good decisions about which patterns might be destructive for you.

One technique I use when I notice myself getting angry is asking myself, "What is the big deal about this? Why is this so important? What do I really have at stake here that is causing me to react so emotionally?" When I begin examining these questions, I usually realize that some deep-seated fear of mine has been triggered—fear of not having enough money, fear of losing something important to me, fear of being hurt all over again.

Moving into Action

1. Make a list of some of the trigger words that cause you to become angry. Say those words to yourself and try to disarm their power.

2. Create a strategy for you to take a time-out when you feel yourself becoming angry.

3. Keep an anger journal in which you list the types of situations that tend to make you angry. Look for patterns. Are there particular people or situations that cause you to blow up—slow drivers, for example, or people who interrupt you while talking? Create an affirmation to help you avoid becoming angered by these people or situations.

3

AVOIDING HOSTILE CONFRONTATIONS

I'm convinced that there is nothing we could do for the world that would be so helpful as to plan on a broad scale for the taming of our anger.

— Neil Clark Warren, *Make Anger Your Ally*

Diffusing Other People's Anger

MANY OF US SPEND TIME AROUND ANGRY PEOPLE. Some of them are occasionally angry, and others are habitually angry. We live and work with people who are volatile, passive, or retaliatory in their expression of anger. They may lash out at us, putting us down. We may also witness people being angry at others in our presence. This is often confusing and upsetting, and we may not know how to respond. Keep in mind that every angry person is different, and every situation is different. There are, however, strategies that you can use to help you when these situations occur.

Let's say John, your boss, is continually yelling about Larry's lack of productivity. You have several choices. You could ask John to discuss his reactions to Larry's work in private. You could talk to Larry about his work and try to help him become more productive. You could encourage John to express his frustration with Larry in more calm ways, using "I" statements. Much of this, of course, would depend upon the kind of relationship you have with John and with Larry.

Other methods for coping with an angry person or outburst include:

1. *Ignore it—and it may go away.*
   This depends upon how frequently the outbursts occur and how loud and abusive they are.

2. *Confront it.*

   Let the person who is venting know that you understand she is angry about something. Encourage her to discuss it calmly, in a respectful manner. If she is venting at you, give direct feedback about how you are hearing her venting. Is it appropriate, considerate, timely? Tell her that you would appreciate her feedback if it were presented in a respectful and nonabusive manner.

3. *Leave the situation.*

   If a person is abusively angry and refuses to accept any feedback, you might excuse yourself—and take a walk. Again, if this is your boss and a job you need, this option may not be realistic.

4. *Try to understand the anger.*

   Calmly tell the person that you are concerned about his anger and would like to help him make things right or work something out. You can encourage him to explain more about what he is feeling. He might get in touch with deeper feelings—such as hurt, fear, or sadness—that are the real causes of his anger.

5. *Reassert your rights and boundaries.*

   If you experience another person's anger as abusive or shaming, reassert your rights and boundaries. Let her know that you do not deserve to be hurt or abused. Make clear "I" statements that do not judge her right to be angry, only her way of expressing it and how it affects you. When Tom's sister yelled at him and called him a "lazy slob" because he didn't respond to her request to help with the dishes, Tom told her that he didn't like being called names. He also apologized for not responding to her call for help.

6. *Encourage people with habitual or volatile anger to explore it.*

   Those who are frequently or violently angry should seek counseling or therapy to explore some of the reasons behind their anger and to learn anger management techniques.

7. *Report abusive anger to higher authorities.*

   Let a person in authority know how you feel when the abusively angry person yells or screams. Make sure your report is confidential.

8. *Give the angry person a book to read about anger management.*
   The angry people may find this book or others listed in the bibliography useful in their understanding and managing anger.

9. *Pray.*
   Ask God to intervene in an angry person's life and help her learn to control her anger and calm herself down.

10. *Discuss your feelings about a person's outbursts with trusted others.*
    Family members or coworkers can listen to your expression of feelings, offer objective perspectives on the anger, and help you create a strategy that might help the angry person cope better with his anger.

Anger in the Workplace

Work environments are filled with pressure due to differences in personality, approaches to tasks, and attitudes toward deadlines. Some people at work will have lower tolerances for frustration than others. Angry coworkers might be easier to deal with than angry bosses. An angry boss has the power to fire you, write a bad recommendation, or make life difficult for you on the job. It takes patience and tact to deal with an angry boss. Use clear "I" statements if your boss is angry at you, and encourage him or her to treat you with respect and kindness.

If a boss is consistently angry to the point of abusiveness, there are harassment guidelines that can be consulted, along with policies and procedures for dealing with it. Timing is important. Don't confront your boss in front of others. Wait until you have gotten over your hurt or anger at the way you feel you have been treated. Be logical and low-key in your confrontation, but be firm.

Sometimes, an organization has an angry corporate culture. If you believe that the anger is getting in the way of your productivity, you can discuss this with your superior. You are probably not going to change an angry organization, and you may have to leave it.

Gossiping and other types of passive anger often permeate organizations. Martha noticed that several members of her work group were always making jokes about Nicole behind her back. Some coworkers seemed envious of Nicole's appearance. She confronted the group about the negative comments and put-downs. She presented factual information, using "I" statements about her feelings of discomfort. She told them that she would not participate in such discussions. After a while, the comments ceased.

Anger in the Family

Family members living together often have squabbles due to close quarters and differences in personalities. Siblings become angry at one another. Parents express anger at their children when chores are not completed. Parents may disagree and express anger at each other. Some families, as we have said, are more tolerant of outbursts than others.

A habitually angry family member can disrupt the entire family. Parents have the responsibility to vent anger privately and considerately and to set guidelines for the appropriate expression of anger within the family setting. If a child is always angry, parents may want to explore other issues, such as depression, a learning disability, or a personality disorder, with a professional counselor. The Rogers family, for example, discovered that their son Kevin had a short temper because he found reading difficult. Once his learning disability was treated, Kevin was less angry and frustrated at home.

Les Carter and Frank Minirth, in *The Anger Workbook,* suggest ways parents can deal with their child's anger. Children will naturally express anger due to frustrations they experience in everyday life, including coping with adult authority. Young children are self-centered and want to have things their own way. They often become angry when parents impose limits and restrictions upon their behavior. Some parents fear their children's anger and get caught in power plays where children whine and complain or threaten to have temper tantrums. In all cases, parents must reiterate the rules without yelling, preaching, or threatening. Parents must not let their children control them through manipulation. The answer is to come up with logical consequences for rule violations and let children know these in advance.

However, it is important to accept the reality that growing up and maturing involves loss, giving in, and compromise. Children and adolescents will be angry as they go through the phases of maturation. It is vital that parents pick their battles and refuse to fight over trivial matters.

Moving into Action

1. Practice making "I" statements when you do not like the way others have expressed or vented their anger. "I feel uncomfortable when you . . ."

2. Make a list of three people in your life who are often angry. How do they express it? How does it affect you? Develop a strategy of positive ways of confronting them about their anger.

3. Create a discipline strategy for your children in which rules are clearly stated and logical consequences exist. Write down some guidelines for healthy anger expression in your household.

4. Encourage others to keep an anger journal or diary and write down the particular situations and people that tend to make them angry and their response. Suggest that they look for patterns.

Coping with Road Rage

Angry people are everywhere—at home, at the office, on the highway. The roads are more crowded these days, and people seem to be more angry on our roadways. The Coalition for Consumer Health and Safety states that 64 percent of Americans believe drivers in their communities are less courteous and safe than five years ago. Road rage has become a national problem. We are concerned for our safety. How often have you experienced it?

I experience road rage daily. Here is one example: It has been a long day. I am tired from teaching classes and meeting with students. I have to rush home to meet a battling couple for counseling. I am not looking forward to seeing them. I am running late. I am stopped, waiting to get onto Interstate 94. The light takes forever to change to green. Just as my light changes, the car in the next lane scoots ahead of me and cuts me off. He is clearly wrong. It wasn't his turn. I am furious because he could have hit my car. I'm lucky he didn't. I want to get back at him after I'm on the freeway. I want to pass him and give him a sign of displeasure. But I stop myself. He may have a gun. He has a bigger car than mine. I had better use my maturity and let it go. I see him weaving in and out of traffic, cutting other people off. I realize it wasn't personal. That's just who he is.

Road ragers are everywhere—from the big cities to the small towns to the rural areas. These drivers are often dangerous; they threaten our safety and our very lives. When I drive at the speed limit, there is often someone tailgating me. Drivers have cut me off. Drivers have refused to let me merge into traffic. I have heard drivers curse and have received digital gestures of displeasure. Have you?

In his *USA Weekend* article "Putting the Brakes on Road Rage," Dennis McCafferty says that Americans drive more aggressively due to anger, stress, impatience, and competitiveness. He says, "Take legions of commuters squeezed for time, add a mentality that says the driver inside your car is always right, and the scene is set for aggression."

While we would like to educate those overly rageful and aggressive drivers about the errors of their ways, we are not going to accomplish very much while moving at sixty or seventy miles per hour. The best advice about dealing with drivers experiencing road rage is to:

1. Get out of their way. If a driver is tailgating you, move to another lane. Make every effort to steer clear.

2. Avoid making any eye contact or gestures that could be interpreted as hostile.

3. Refrain from honking your horn.

4. Back off if they cut you off. Don't let them know they wronged you. They won't care, and they might try to hurt you.

5. Report aggressive drivers to the authorities by providing a vehicle description, license plate number, location, and the direction of travel.

6. Pray for their recovery.

7. Pray for other drivers who are harassed by road ragers.

8. Keep *your* anger in check on the road.

Curbing road rage will take a national effort, better law enforcement, and some spiritual healing.

Moving into Action

1. Devise a plan for coping with a hostile and aggressive tailgater. Have you been speeding up or moving out of the way?

2. What are some words you can say to yourself to calm yourself down when you experience someone who is rageful on the roads?

3. Is there something you can do in your community to make the local police more alert to the problem of road rage?

4. When you are impatient behind the wheel, what can you do or say that will relax or destress you? Try "I am not in that much of a hurry. I will get there. I don't have to worry if I am a few minutes late."

4

LEARNING TO DESTRESS YOURSELF

The acute stresses of life produce temporary physiological responses from which the body recovers. It's the chronic stresses that are the real challenge to healing.

— Joan Borysenko, *Minding the Body, Mending the Mind*

Learning to Relax

STRESS IS ONE OF THE LEADING CAUSES OF ANGER. People who try to do too much, who feel overloaded and undervalued, may become angry. Angry people are often tense. Tense people sometimes become angry. One way to cope with a tendency to become angry easily is to learn how to relax, take a time-out, and clear one's head. *Dr. Sehnert's New Guide to Managing Your Stress* offers many suggestions for lowering your stress. Let's consider five of them here:

1. *Lessen the amount of stimulation you experience.*
   Most of us live with others and work with others. We are crowded in. We fight to be heard. We fight for parking places. We fight for our rightful place on the highways. To destress and relax, we can reduce the amount of stimulation in our environment. This might mean driving on a side street instead of the freeway. It may mean staying in a small bed and breakfast instead of a large hotel. Try turning off the TV or the radio. Giving ourselves transition time for activities can also help us concentrate on the task at hand. When we run quickly from one thing to another, we don't leave enough time to process what we have experienced and refuel our energy for the next activity.

2. *Eliminate some of your activities.*
   Some people destress by simplifying their lives. They realize that they cannot keep going at the pace they have been. They know something has to give. Figuring out what you can leave out is a challenge. For some, it means not serving on a committee. For others, it means spending less time with extended family. Or it might mean setting more realistic goals at work and giving themselves more time to work on existing projects before taking on new ones.

3. *Find quiet places where you can retreat.*
   For some people, destressing means being alone. When you get away from everyone else, you can get away from distractions, expectations, and demands. This time alone can not only help you relax and calm down, but can also give you an opportunity to explore your true feelings and your true calling. For some people, being alone helps them put things into perspective. Anthony Storr, author of *Solitude: A Return to the Self,* believes that alone time gives you a chance to access your own inner wisdom. There you are able to sort out ideas, change attitudes, and integrate new experiences into your life.

   Some people hesitate to spend time alone because they associate it with being unpopular. They may be afraid they would be too bored. But alone time provides opportunity to be more absorbed in the moment. Quiet meditation time can help you focus on your body, your thoughts, your needs, and your purpose. In solitude, you can to come to terms with your losses, fears, and desires.

   There are people who become angry when they believe they are continually trying to please others. They may put on a mask and live the way they think others want them to live. Then after a while, they may become resentful of the way they are catering to others and explode in anger. When people are alone, they put less energy into pretending and pleasing and more into feeling and being. They may even decide that the masks they wear are unnecessary.

   Barbara, a single mother, has two children. Every few months, she leaves her children with her sister, Karen, and drives to Clare's Well, a retreat center about an hour away. Barbara spends two days resting, journaling, reading, and walking in the woods. When she returns, she has usually sorted out something that has been bothering her. She is eager to see her children, and she feels like a new person. The children notice the difference in Barbara and also enjoy spending time with their aunt.

There are many retreat centers that offer places for quiet solitude and reflection. Consider going somewhere for a day or two for rejuvenation.

4. *Get in touch with your feelings.*
Many excessively angry people are not in touch with their other feelings. They don't take the time and space to quiet themselves, think, meditate, and pray. They ignore signals from their bodies that they are too tired, too full of food, too stretched in too many directions. The key to healing anger is to get off the treadmill and notice what is going on in your mind, body, emotions, and spiritual life.

Getting in touch can involve journaling, writing down thoughts and feelings. Other people might benefit from talking into a tape recorder and rambling for a while. Still others need to find one special person with whom to spend some quality quiet time.

5. *Take better care of your body.*
Most angry people would benefit from a regular exercise program where they sweat and elevate their heart rate. Some people find that standing on their head, a centuries-old yoga technique, alleviates stress. Pay attention to what you eat. Watch your caffeine, fat, and sugar intake. Change your eating habits for a week and see if you feel better. When you eat, eat slowly. Don't eat and watch television, or eat and drive. Enjoy the sensual pleasure of food, and you will eat less. Take a hot bubble bath by candlelight. Take a daily walk in the woods. Pay attention to your breathing. Try to slow your breathing down. Relaxing your body is a necessity, not a luxury.

Learning the ways that you can destress will help you slow your life down and give you more time to think, savor what you have, count your blessings, and enjoy each and every day.

Moving into Action

1. Check out local exercise programs and yoga classes. Sign up for one.

2. Look for quiet places in your area or retreat centers that focus on holistic healing. Go away for a day or two by yourself.

3. Buy a journal or notebook and start writing down your thoughts and feelings.

4. Keep a list of the foods you eat that have an excess of sugar, fat, or caffeine. Try to eat more fruits and vegetables.

5. Develop a destressing routine before you go to bed at night. Take a short walk, or take a long, relaxing bubble bath.

6. Focus on your breathing, holding your breath, and then letting it out slowly.

7. Tighten and tense up your muscles and then relax them one by one, breathing deeply as you do.

8. Stretch every part of you every day.

Once you are relaxed, you will find that you have more energy to carry on with your life. Little things won't make you stressed and angry.

Finding Peaceful Role Models

Another way to heal anger is to find peaceful role models. Peaceful role models help us destress by setting a good example. People who seem to take things in stride, who seem calm, peaceful, and relaxed as they go about their business, generally have a sense of self that is stable and consistent. They don't seem to be swayed by their emotions or by external events. They can go through a stormy experience and still maintain a level of calm. These role models have trust in the world—things will get done, everything ultimately will be all right. They are not arrogant or rude. They tend to bounce back from disappointments and hardships.

How do we find these people? We need to keep our eyes open as we engage in our daily routines. Once we find them, we don't have to interview them to discover their secret. We just have to use them as an example, a plumb line showing us how we should try to behave.

Does it really rub off? I believe that when we spend time with aggressive and hostile people, we tend to be more aggressive and hostile ourselves as a defense. When we find calm and relaxed people, we are allowed to let down our defenses and be who we are. This can give help us be peaceful and calm.

People who are slow to anger are frequently spiritual in nature. They have found something greater than themselves and gain a sense of strength and calm from this outside source. For Christians, Jesus' message of God's grace gives them a sense of comfort and calm. People who know they are loved despite their imperfections don't have to run around proving themselves. They don't beat themselves up when they make mistakes. Anxiety, fear, and self-doubt can lead to anger. Spiritual people seem to be less anxious, less fearful, and more self-assured because they know that they are truly loved just as they are. Some of these spiritual people can be found in churches. Others can be found on mountaintops or at retreat centers. And still others can be found within the communities in which we live.

There is no set formula of where to look. Just keep looking, and pay attention. You will find them.

Moving into Action

1. List three people you already know who could be described as peaceful role models.

2. List five things you have learned from these peaceful people.

3. List three places where you will look for additional role models.

4. What are three behaviors you can demonstrate that would make you a good role model?

Developing a Loving Support Group

One of the best ways to help heal anger is to develop a loving support group of people who genuinely care about you. This means, of course, that you have to genuinely care about them. You can help create a support group in a church setting, or you can develop an informal group of support people as friends. How does a support group help heal anger?

1. A support group cares about you in times of need and trouble. You can rely on them to be interested, to listen, and to provide helpful suggestions.

2. A support group gives you an opportunity to vent your feelings, especially anger, expressing them in a safe, caring environment.

3. A support group can help you see the larger picture. They can provide suggestions, options, and alternatives.

4. You learn to forgive yourself and others in a support-group setting. Since supporters create a caring, nurturing place, they accept people with their limitations and weaknesses.

5. A group can help you see that everyone encounters problems and difficult situations. You realize that you are not alone, and you may realize that you are seeing your situation in ways that are out of proportion with reality.

6. You can learn coping skills in a group and benefit from other people's experiences. As you see how others have handled tough situations, you can benefit from their wisdom.

It takes effort and motivation to develop a supportive network of caring people, but it is worth the energy. Your anger will dissipate when you realize that you have the help and support you need to cope with life's crises. You will discover that you can more easily let go of your anger if you believe that others, in the support group, have heard you and taken you seriously.

To develop a support group, carefully select people who might be interested. Because support groups involve trust, choose people who you already believe you can trust. Some formal support groups meet regularly. How often you meet can be determined by your schedule and the schedules of others in your group. Spiritual support groups are sometimes called prayer groups. These may also involve readings, Scripture, and discussions of spirituality and spiritual growth. Some churches already have spiritual support groups you can join.

Moving into Action

1. List several possible support groups you could join.

2. List a few friends who might be part of your support network.

3. List four qualities that you believe are crucial to have in a support network if you are going to trust the people in it.

Finding Trustworthy Helpers

Adding to our anger today are the annoyances we experience when we take our cars in to be fixed or when the clerk hands us the wrong prescription refill. People who provide services for us will make mistakes. However, some built-up anger comes from trusting service people who are inconsistent and untrustworthy. In order to lessen our anger, it is important to find competent, reliable people to help take care of our various needs. We can find a network of trustworthy automobile dealers and mechanics, doctors, lawyers, hair stylists, cleaners, dentists, financial planners, and others.

In all the time I knew him, my father always bought his cars from one dealer. I wondered why he never comparison shopped. When I asked him about this, he told me that once you find someone you believe you can really trust, you should stick with that person. You are paying a small premium for considerate, consistent, and reliable service, he told me. I have taken his advice. I look for service people whom I believe I can trust.

This lessens my anger and frustration because I don't have to be concerned about being let down by these people. They will do what they say they will do, and they will do it politely and considerately. Finding the right people to provide you with service can take years and involve some disappointments. How can this process be facilitated?

1. Get recommendations from other people and follow up on them.

2. Look for people who keep their promises and commitments.

3. Look for people who willing to "go the extra mile" to provide good service.

4. Interview several people before you choose one to do the job.

5. Pay attention to service people when you interview them. Are they accurate, kind, and forthright in their approach?

6. Support small business owners if you can; they have a direct stake in serving you well.

7. State your wishes clearly when you engage someone's help. Specifically ask for what you want, and state when you would like the work to be completed.

8. Complain respectfully if the job is not done right. Pay attention to how your complaint is handled.

9. Notice whether service providers apologize when they make a mistake. Find those who are not afraid to admit their imperfections and yet try to do the best job possible.

10. Be a good and loyal customer. If people do something well for you, let them know you appreciate their service.

If you have a network of people you trust to provide necessary services, you can go about the business of living with purpose and making a difference. You will have less stress and therefore less anger.

Moving into Action

On a scale of one to ten, with ten being excellent, rate the trustworthiness, competence, and reliability of your service providers.

_____	Doctor	_____	Lawyer
_____	Day Care Provider	_____	Clothing Salesperson
_____	Baby-sitter	_____	Dentist
_____	Lawn Service Provider	_____	Therapist or Counselor
_____	Auto Mechanic	_____	Financial Planner
_____	Real Estate Agent	_____	Car Dealer
_____	Plumber	_____	Electrician
_____	Chiropractor	_____	Pharmacist
_____	Hair Stylist	_____	Cleaners
_____	Travel Agent	_____	Others

5

INSTILLING IN YOURSELF REALISTIC ATTITUDES TOWARD LIFE

An impressive study of the sources of well-being of Harvard men at age 65 found that, by that age, their emotional health was not grounded in a happy childhood or awards or other testimonies to a successful career. It was the men who had developed the resilience to absorb life's shocks and conflicts—without passivity, blaming, bitterness, or self-destructive behaviors—who were best able to enjoy their third act. . . . Instead of lashing out in anger or looking for others to blame or retreating into depression when faced with emotional crisis, they have learned to sleep on major decisions and to wait until they can respond in a calm, measured way.

— Gail Sheehy, *Understanding Men's Passages*

Developing Realistic Expectations

W E KNOW THAT ANGER often comes from having unrealistic expectations of ourselves, others, and life. In this chapter, we will learn how to change those unrealistic expectations into more realistic ones.

In order to become more realistic about life and people, it helps to understand the concept of acceptance. Acceptance means that we don't expect perfection from people, and we don't expect everything to always go our way. Coming to terms with life's complexities and disappointments and with people's limitations prevents a lot of anger.

Many of us grew up idealistic about our capabilities to improve the world. We were going to change things for the better. Our generation was going to make the big difference. But the truth we discovered is that life is difficult and presents more problems than solutions. Idealism is a good motivator, but too much idealism can lead to anger and resentment when reality hits.

Having realistic expectations means accepting the following:

1. Nothing lasts forever, except God.
2. Life is made up of joys and sorrows, successes and disappointments.
3. Everyone is imperfect and limited in some way.
4. Even though we may try our hardest, we will sometimes fall short. We need to constantly forgive ourselves in advance for our human limitations.
5. We can learn to bounce back when hard things happen.
6. It is difficult to discern who can really be trusted. Even the most trustworthy friend may occasionally disappoint us. Similarly, people in power are sometimes untrustworthy, and sometimes they deceive themselves.
7. The love you send out may not be returned to you in the same way.
8. Not everyone will like you no matter how likeable you are.
9. Not everything you read or hear should be believed.
10. Media and advertising promise us things that are not true. The messages are designed to get to us to buy things that we think will improve our lives. Some of them will, and some of them won't.

How do we learn to let go of our notions of perfection about ourselves and others? We tell ourselves that life is okay, but not perfect. Good things will happen, but bad things will happen, too. Life is in control (God's control, not ours).

When I am frustrated with a situation, I try to define my expectations. Usually my frustration is a sign that I am being unrealistic and demanding. Perhaps I expect perfect service in a restaurant and don't receive it. I could then be mad about it, or I could accept that waiters and waitresses are limited, fallible human beings. Some of them will try to do a good job and will indeed do their best. However, the service won't always be perfect.

The steps to developing realistic expectations about life and people include:

1. Don't judge according to an extremely high standard.

2. Learn to be content with imperfect people and situations.

3. Develop a 10 percent grace factor. (According to Jennifer James in *Success is the Quality of Your Journey,* 10 percent of the time people will hurt or disappoint you. Accept that reality.)

4. Learn to be patient when you are required to wait.

5. Develop self-talk that reminds you that life is going to work out fine, even if there are some bumps in the road.

6. Recognize that failure is part of living and part of growing. As Kofi Anan, secretary general of the United Nations, said in a commencement address at Macalester College in St. Paul, Minnesota (May 1998), if you have failed, you probably haven't pushed something hard enough.

7. Appreciate the times when things go well and on schedule.

8. Make the most of each day—and try to live in the moment rather than anticipating what could go wrong.

9. Spend time with people who are homeless or poor, ill or dying, who have it much worse than you do. You may gain perspective on what really matters in people and life.

10. Slow down and relax. If you don't get everything done today, it will be there waiting for you tomorrow.

Letting go of our need to control life and our perfectionism is one of the most important ways to calm our anger. On a day when we are in the biggest hurry, we will probably get stuck behind a slow driver who seems like he or she has the whole day to get somewhere. On the day when we are at our stress limit, we may be handed one more thing to do. People who accept life as it is, with its limits and imperfections, don't get thrown by curveballs. They expect zigs and zags and adjust accordingly. The qualities that are most important in minimizing anger and maintaining a positive attitude are flexibility and resilience. People who are flexible and resilient roll with the punches.

Moving into Action

1. List several disappointments you have experienced over the last five years.

2. List six television programs that do not present life realistically.

3. Agree in your family to limit the amount of television and commercial watching and see if anger diminishes in your household.

4. Write down an unrealistic expectation that you have of someone else. How can you turn it into a realistic expectation?

5. Write a positive affirmation about your own ability to handle the difficulties in real life situations.

6. List five joys that you have experienced over the last five years.

7. Implement the 10 percent grace factor into your daily life—acknowledging that 10 percent of the time you will be disappointed, late, or have to deal with difficult people.

Grieving Losses and Disappointments

Ridding ourselves of our perfectionism and unrealistic expectations is one kind of letting go. Another kind is grieving the losses and disappointments we all experience in our lives. Some of these hurts are caused by others, through rejection or put-downs. Some people hurt us intentionally, while others hurt us unintentionally. Some hurts we bring on ourselves. Others are just the result of living life.

As we grow older, we lose some of our capabilities. We may lose our hair, our keen eyesight, our excellent hearing. Friends and relatives, our loved ones, move away or die. We may have to give up something important to us—a childhood blanket, a job, or a home lost to a hurricane, flood, or tornado. Loss is a part of life, and loss hurts. Many people respond to losses with anger. Joan Borysenko, author of *Minding the Body, Mending the Mind,* points out that anger is a natural response to hurt.

According to Elizabeth Kübler-Ross, author of *Death: A Final Stage of Growth,* anger is an important stage in the grieving process. The initial response to loss, the first stage in the process, is shock. Then some people want to deny that the loss has occurred. The next stage is the anger stage—"Why me? This isn't fair." Then comes depression, followed by bargaining, trying to get back what one has lost by making some kind of pact or deal with God. And finally, there is the acceptance of the loss and reintegrating one's life. Yet sometimes people stay stuck in the anger stage and wallow in it, not moving onto sadness, bargaining, and acceptance.

People who wallow in anger may respond differently. Some people bottle up their anger and keep it inside. Others vent it violently, attacking other people. Still others use their anger as a way of isolating themselves. Borysenko believes that we must learn how to let go of our anger. She writes: "The tragedy is that the anger remains long after any positive learning can come out of it. Some of us are still nursing grudges against people who have been dead for years."

Focusing on anger and remaining angry may shut off other emotions that are a necessary part of the grieving process. Anger can become part of a person's identity. "If I am not angry, then I do not know who I am." Some people believe they need to stay angry as a sign of loyalty to a loved one who has died. Others direct their anger at doctors, the police, investigators, or funeral directors. Some people feel guilty if they don't stay stuck in their anger. Some people may need professional help to move past anger and through the remaining grief stages. A good support group or therapist can aid in giving permission and a safe place to feel all the complicated feelings involved in a loss. In order to move past anger, people need to:

1. Face the reality of their loss and allow themselves to feel sad.

2. Understand that they are not alone in their loss.

3. Look beyond or beneath the anger at their pain and the other losses they have experienced in the past.

4. Open themselves to healing.

5. Accept life, with all of its losses and disappointments.

6. Surrender spiritually to God or some higher power.

7. Believe that some learning will come out of this pain and sorrow.

Jeff, a friend of mine, has grieved the loss of his father who had Alzheimer's disease. He has dedicated an hour a week to help others who have Alzheimer's as a way of remembering his father and celebrating his life. Sandra had a difficult time cleaning out her mother's closets after she died. She didn't want to throw away or give away her mother's dresses. After stewing about it for a while, she decided to keep five of them and made them into a quilt, which she later hung on her wall.

Moving into Action

Write down the answers to the following:

1. Make a list of some of the losses you have experienced in the last five years.

2. Which losses caused you to feel the most anger?

3. Have you let go of the anger you felt during those losses?

4. How did you feel when you did let go of your anger?

5. Is it difficult for you to let go? Why do you think so?

6. Have you gone through the different grief stages with each one of the losses?

7. What grief work do you believe you still have to do?

8. Write a letter to someone you have lost either to death or the ending of a relationship, expressing the wide range of feelings about what he or she meant to you.

Recognizing Guilt As a Form of Anger

In *Minding the Body, Mending the Mind,* Joan Borysenko discusses guilt as a kind of anger. She notes that guilt makes us feel bad and results in other reactions. Guilt is a form of self-anger. But that anger can spill over onto others. We can blame other people for our feelings and thus avoid those feelings.

Holding onto resentments makes some people feel superior. Borysenko believes that "most of us are carrying around a lot of unnecessary baggage full of guilt and resentment. Often the people who are most critical of other people's behavior are those who are most critical of themselves."

In order to let go of resentments and guilt, people must learn to accept life as imperfect. We must learn to forgive ourselves and others for mistakes. According to Borysenko, forgiveness starts with ourselves and then extends to others. She suggests that people make a list of their regrets and resentments. She encourages people to make phone calls, write letters, offer apologies, and make amends for things they are sorry they did. Finally, she believes that people need to honor themselves and others.

Terry has finally let go of the dream she had for her marriage. She and Mark divorced two years ago. She claimed that the divorce forced her to realize that her hope that Mark would change was unrealistic. She is now ready to move on with her life.

None of us will have the perfect life. Many of us will struggle to accomplish something we believe to be worthwhile and then have it either be unrecognized or trivialized. Accepting losses and hurt as part of living requires maturity, empathy, and humility.

Moving into Action

1. List several past behaviors about which you still feel guilty. Write a brief letter of forgiveness to yourself.

2. Write down something that you have done in the past for which you believe you should apologize. Write a letter of apology to the person you offended. Send the letter if you feel doing so is appropriate.

Understanding Collective, Societal Grieving

While individuals can be helped emotionally and spiritually to grieve and move on, collective, societal anger is harder to resolve, because not all people are willing to let go and grow spiritually. When a larger society is involved in anger due to loss—for example, over the death of President Kennedy, Martin Luther King Jr., Princess Diana—the media often fuels the anger by continuing to bring it up, then oversimplifying it.

Moving past collective, societal anger can be done when most people decide they have been mad long enough and they now need to be sad. Then, they can finally accept the reality that loss is a part of life. Letting go of illusions and idealism helps a person or a society move on.

Perhaps a lot of anger that our society displays comes from that lack of maturity and understanding about the complexity of life. If we expect things always to go well, we will be hurt, frustrated, and disappointed when they do not. We may look around for someone to blame. Mistakes, problems, and struggles can be seen as someone's fault. If we believe in retaliation, an eye for an eye, we can begin to think about how to get back at someone who has hurt or wronged us.

Anger is only helpful if it is acknowledged, dealt with, and ultimately released. Our anger can tell us many things about ourselves and life. Situations where we are hurt or frustrated can become lessons for us to learn. If we are willing to see them as lessons, we will be less likely to want to retaliate and hurt others.

Moving into Action

1. What political or social events of the last few decades do you believe people are still angry about? What could be done to help society let go of its anger?

2. Write a personal resolution promising that you will avoid participating in unconstructive collective hostility about social problems.

Developing a Forgiving Attitude

We grieve losses and hurts. Releasing these allows us to forgive, and forgiveness enables us to move on from the past. When we forgive, a weight is lifted from us. It is physically, spiritually, and emotionally healthy to forgive.

An article in the April 5, 1999, issue of *Time* titled "Should All Be Forgiven?" reports that psychologist Everett Worthington and others claim that forgiveness dissipates anger, mends marriages, and banishes depression. In part, the article describes research—sponsored by the Worthington-directed Templeton Foundation Campaign for Forgiveness Research—into the physiological effects of forgiveness. One professor involved in such research, Charlotte Van Oyen Witvliet of Hope College, placed electrodes on a young volunteer. The volunteer would remember a hurt that has been done to him and nurse a grudge. He would then hear a cue that tells him to shift gears and empathize with the offender, imagining ways of wishing the person well. Heart rate, blood pressure, sweat, and muscle tension were measured. In the process, Witvliet found great physiological differences between forgiving and unforgiving states. Stress, she discovered, is significantly higher when revenge is considered.

Witvliet believes that people might hold onto grudges because it makes them feel more in control. In reality, however, subjects reported a greater sense of control when they empathized and an even greater sense of control when they granted forgiveness. In her study of seventy subjects, both men and women, Witvliet has found that maintaining grudges encourages the build-up of anger. To let go of that anger, she and other researchers encourage, people need to forgive.

Time also described how forgiveness research has been done with cancer patients, incest survivors, and parents whose adult children have ignored them for years. In all cases, forgiveness lessened the amount of stress and the amount of anger research subjects felt. There were noticeable physiological changes.

In their book *Forgiveness,* Sidney and Suzanne Simon write about how forgiveness relates to healing. They claim that forgiveness is:

- a by-product of an ongoing healing process.
- an internal process.
- a sign of positive self-esteem.
- letting go of the intense emotions attached to incidents from our past.
- recognizing that we no longer need our grudges and resentments, our hatred and self-pity.
- no longer wanting to punish the people who hurt us.
- accepting that nothing we do to punish them will heal us.
- freeing up and putting to better use the energy once consumed by holding grudges, harboring resentments, and nursing unhealed wounds.
- moving on.

When people store up anger and resentment due to past hurts, say the Simons, they hurt themselves by not moving forward. They identify six different healing phases of the forgiveness recovery process. The first phase is denial, where we refuse to believe that what has hurt us makes much difference. The second phase, self-blame, assumes that we were responsible for the negative things that happened to us. In the third phase, victim, we realize we were not to blame for what happened and may wallow in self-pity or lash out in anger at anyone else who "crosses" us. In the fourth phase, indignation, we are angry and intolerant; we become self-righteous and want to retaliate. In the fifth phase, survivor, we recognize that we survived despite the horrible things that happened to us. The Simons say that in this phase we become aware of our strengths and welcome the return of compassion. The sixth and final phase, integration, allows us to acknowledge the wounds and limitations of those who hurt us. We release them from prison and reclaim the energy we have used to keep them there. We don't ever forget what happened and we don't condone it. We just let it go.

People can go through these phases as individuals or as a society. In looking at the United States today, we can identify that much of the culture is going through the victim and indignation phases. It seems few people have entered into phases five and six.

As people work through the six phases, they acknowledge the pain and suffering they have received and learn that they did not deserve it. At the same time, they move beyond the grudges and self-righteousness to an acceptance of what happened and to forgiveness. Many people realize they have become stronger, more independent, more spiritually connected due to the suffering they have experienced.

Forgiveness requires time, self-awareness, and a desire to let it go. Some people want to let it go because they realize that they are being weighed down by their own resentments and anger. Maintaining resentments, according to the Simons, gives people a sense of power. If they are generally feeling powerless about their lives, holding onto grudges may give them the only sense of power they have.

One of the most interesting reasons for holding grudges, the authors believe, is that people have the illusion that if the bad things hadn't happened, they would have had the "perfect" life. The Simons confirm our notion that anger results from having unrealistic expectations about life and people.

Robert Veninga, in *A Gift of Hope: How We Survive Our Tragedies*, writes that "human pain does not let go of its grip at one point in time. Rather it works its way out of our consciousness over time. There is a season of sadness. A season of anger. A season of tranquility. A season of hope." Sometimes we have to help the season of anger along by letting go of our grudges and intentionally reaching out to others and forgiving them.

Mary, for instance, has felt slighted by her sister-in-law, Fran. At a family gathering, Fran did not even acknowledge Mary's presence. Mary was extremely hurt by this, but said nothing. A year later, when Mary brought Fran a birthday gift, Fran put it on the floor and never sent Mary a written thank-you note for the gift. For sixteen years, Mary has nursed a grudge and has decided to cut Fran out of her life. She has bitter feelings toward Fran. She avoids family gatherings where Fran is present. When asked why Mary continues to hold this grudge against her, Mary says she doesn't want to be vulnerable to Fran. She's afraid she will be hurt again.

Over the years, Mary has become a cynical and isolated person. Her unforgiving attitude toward Fran has spread to the ways she feels about other family members. Mary's son, Tom, asked her to consider forgiving Fran, talking to her, and attending Easter dinner with the whole family. At first, Mary did not want to do it. She protested. It was though she'd have to give up a part of herself.

Tom told her that forgiving Fran would not mean that what Fran did to her was right. It would not be an admission that the hurt didn't occur, he said; what she did still was wrong. It would simply be for the sake of Mary that she forgive, so she can move on with her life. Mary decided to talk to Fran and told her how she had been feeling. Fran apologized and said she had no idea that she had hurt Mary so badly. She promised to be more aware in the future of her behavior and how it affects others. Mary did go to the family dinner at Easter and felt a new life being born within her. She laughed and joked with extended family members for the first time in years.

Just as venting might increase anger and hostility, thinking negative thoughts about someone and holding onto a grudge might also increase anger. Developing a forgiving attitude and letting go of grudges heals anger. We can learn to forgive ourselves for our mistakes, others for the things they have done to us, and life for not being perfect. This forgiving attitude is helpful in calming us down and moving us into the present and future, rather than keeping us stuck in the past.

Moving into Action

1. List the names of several people you still need to forgive. What is keeping you from forgiving them?

2. Write a forgiveness letter (you may choose to send it or not) to someone who you have been unwilling to forgive in the past.

3. What can you forgive of yourself? What have you done wrong that you are holding against yourself? Write yourself a letter of forgiveness.

4. Develop a forgiving attitude. Decide to let small hurts go, and forgive life for being less than perfect on a daily basis. Keep a record of the little disappointments, hurts, and slights that no longer make you angry.

Developing a Feeling of Gratitude

Along with a forgiving attitude, a feeling of gratitude for the blessings in your life helps to dissipate anger. If people keep in mind that they are very blessed, they tend to become less angry when others don't live up to their expectations. Grateful people are less likely to feel slighted or hold grudges. An attitude of gratitude and compassion allows us to be free of comparisons. We no longer have to be the ones who set the standards, make the rules, or try to control other people.

Grateful people count their blessings every day and appreciate the good things that have happened in their lives. They realize that some of the hardships were good learning experiences and frequently brought them to a new understanding of life, themselves, and others.

Moving into Action

1. List ten blessings for which you are grateful.

2. List two difficult situations that you endured that taught you valuable life lessons.

6

NOURISHING YOURSELF THROUGH SPIRITUAL RESOURCES

The trusting child does not have a worry in the world about whether he is smart enough, or handsome enough, whether he has accomplished enough with his life, or been good enough to be acceptable to his parent. He trusts that the someone who holds him, warms him, feeds him, cradles him, and loves him will accept him again and always. Trust is the inner child we discover in an experience of grace.

— Lewis B. Smedes, *Shame and Grace*

Using the Bible to Calm Your Anger

As we have discussed, one of the causes of an angry society is a lack of spiritual connectedness felt by its people. The Bible can be an excellent place to start forming a more meaningful spiritual and spiritually connected life because the Bible offers lessons for living. These lessons create a more calm and serene life. What follows is a summary of some of the main biblical messages that can lead to calming our anger.

1. *God's grace means we are loved despite our imperfections.*
   This frees us from perfectionism and the need to be in control. Because we are loved as we are, we need not experience the added pressure and stress of seeking the approval of human beings. With less stress, we feel less anger.

2. *We are to accept our imperfections and live humbly.*
   The Bible teaches us to accept our imperfections and live humbly, with little pride and arrogance. Anger often comes out of a need to be right. When we lose this need, anger dissipates. We can learn from the Bible that life will not be easy and we should not expect life to give us everything we want right away.

3. *We are not alone when we rely on God.*
   When we learn to rely on God to help us solve our problems, we no longer feel the stress of being alone. We know we can depend upon God to take care of us and help us in times of trouble. With more trust and less fear, we are not as threatened by difficult circumstances. We believe that we shall overcome—with God's help.

4. *We are to focus on love, not fear.*
   We are taught through the Commandments to focus on love rather than fear. When we love God, others, and ourselves, we stop worrying about what we are receiving and think more about what we are giving. This attitude of generosity leads to a greater tolerance and acceptance of others and therefore less anger at their limits. We also lose our judgmental anger if we live accepting others as they are.

5. *We are to live in community.*
   God wants us to live in community and concern ourselves with the welfare of others. This other-centered focus keeps us from becoming too self-centered. When we are concerned for others, we are less likely to be self-centered and easily hurt.

6. *We are to use anger positively to seek justice.*
   The Bible teaches us to seek justice and encourages us to turn our anger into positive action. Such positive action might take the form of feeding the poor, helping the sick, or supporting the outcasts. If we follow the Bible's teachings, much of our anger becomes constructive.

By focusing on the central message of the Bible—that God loves us as we are—we can begin to build our spiritual resources. Spiritual healing involves our knowing that we are loved for who we are and accepting God's grace. According to Lewis Smedes, most people experience God's grace as:

- Pardon: we are forgiven for wrongs we have done.
- Acceptance: we are reunited with God and our true selves. We are accepted, cradled, held, affirmed, and loved. Accepting grace is the answer to shame.
- Power: we receive a spiritual energy to shed the heaviness of shame.
- Gratitude: we gain a sense for the gift of life, a sense of wonder, and sometimes elation at the lavish generosity of God.

With grace, we are moved to pardon and accept others. We no longer have to be right, in control, judgmental, critical, or angry. The grace of God transcends space and time and takes us out of the immediate moment of loss or disappointment. It moves us to a more spiritual place, above and beyond the hurts and frustrations of everyday life. As we experience this grace, we can let go of our grudges and our demands for perfection. When we truly know grace, we feel joy and learn to let go of our anger.

Intense, relentless anger seems to be a symptom of a joyless and graceless existence. To overturn anger, one must experience the grace of God and the joy of living. Joy comes from truly knowing that God loves us as we are and forgives us—repeatedly, daily, always. Smedes tells us, "The truth is that if we refuse to feel joy until every problem is solved, every stomach full, every person housed, all violence stopped, we will have no joy on this side of the New Earth. Joy in a world that does not work right must be a generous joy. Joy is always, always in spite of the fact that the whole world is groaning while it waits for its redemption."

Moving into Action

How can you learn learn to feel God's grace?

1. Pray about it, asking God to pour divine love into your heart.

2. Write words that convince yourself that you are lovable despite your imperfections.

3. Surround yourself with people who also feel God's grace.

4. Make a list of all the second chances you have had in your life and of how God has been with you through your mistakes.

5. Begin trying to model God's forgiveness by forgiving others for their limits and shortcomings.

6. Let go of your own need to be perfect and your expectation that others be perfect as well.

Relying on Spiritual Guidelines for Support

Spiritual guidelines provide us with the support we need to handle ourselves in an imperfect world. God's unfailing love and grace ground us in a world of ups and downs. We are not lonely because we experience God's presence. We are not fearful because we know we shall overcome any adversity. We are not prideful because we realize that the world is centered around God, not ourselves. We learn to put our trust in God's hands rather than only our own or other people's. While others may provide us with care and support, that is not always enough to handle the difficult situations and suffering in which we find ourselves. Let's look at a few spiritual guidelines.

1. *Develop Realistic Expectations.*
   There are many passages in the Bible that warn us against having unrealistic expectations about life, ourselves, and others. As sinners, we are less than perfect. We can be prideful, arrogant, and prone to disappoint ourselves and others. If we can accept the fallibility of all people, including ourselves, we will not be so disappointed or angry.

2. *Overcome Pride and Arrogance.*
   Our pride and arrogance make us think we can solve problems by ourselves. We believe we are entitled to have what we want. Christ's message is to care about others and be a servant of all. This means that our focus should move from ourselves to the needs and feelings of others. We will be less self-centered and therefore less frustrated when things don't go our way.

3. *Love God, Love Your Neighbor.*
   In Matthew 22:36-39, Jesus names the most important commandments: "Love the Lord your God with all your heart, and with all your soul, and with all your mind," and "you shall love your neighbor as yourself." When we focus on loving God and others rather than on pride and fear, the little things that would annoy, disturb, or bother us becomes less significant. We don't get angry as often because we are not expecting to be pleased or be the focus of attention.

4. *Remember That You Are Resilient.*
   The Bible teaches us that we are resilient and can overcome suffering and disappointment with God's support. We can thrive despite rejections, losses, and suffering. In 2 Timothy 1:7, we are told, "God did not give us a spirit of cowardice, but rather a spirit of power and of love and of self-discipline." We can also learn to manage hurt and rejection and recover from them. Further, God is responsible for the inner strength that keeps us rebounding. In 1 Corinthians 4:7, Paul asks, "What do you have that you did not receive?" God has provided us with skills to handle disappointment and frustration and gives us the inner strength to cope with loss.

5 *Refrain from Judging Others.*
   Given our weaknesses and our limitations, we are not in a position to judge others. Paul says in 2 Corinthians 10:12, "When they measure themselves by one another, and compare themselves with one another, they do not show good sense." God is the judge of human character; we are not.

6. *Trust God.*
   Finally, we need to believe that only God is in charge. In Psalm 56:4, it is written that "in God I trust; I am not afraid; what can flesh do to me?" As we move away from letting other people judge and define us, we feel a new sense of inner peace and freedom.

Moving into Action

1. Write down two unrealistic expectations that you have about life or people. (For example, all people should always do what they say they will do.) Where did these expectations come from?

2. Correct the unrealistic expectation with a more realistic one. (For example, most of the time most people will do what they say they are going to do.)

3. Tell yourself, "I don't have to rely solely on myself or other people. God will support me and help me in times of need."

4. Commit to spending time each week doing things for others who are less fortunate than you are.

5. Keep track of how many times you profess your love for God in a day or in a week. Consider making that profession more often.

6. Keep a faith diary listing your faith-motivated actions and the thoughts and concerns you have for others.

7. Remind yourself that you are a resilient person who can recover from hurt, suffering, and disappointment.

8. List several times when you have been resilient.

9. Start imagining yourself as a resilient person. Say, "With God's help, I am resilient."

10. When you notice yourself judging or criticizing others, stop and remind yourself that God is the only judge.

11. When others criticize you, realize that they are sharing only their perspective. Don't give their criticism so much power that it overwhelms or demoralizes you.

12. Detach yourself from highly critical and judgmental people.

Developing a Personal Sense of Purpose

Anger often arises when we place too much stock in others and too much in ourselves. Our pride, arrogance, and dependency on people lead us astray. We have too much at stake and try to live up to an ideal that is impossible. We become unrealistic about ourselves and others. Anger builds because we are too vulnerable to other human beings. We try too hard to be in control and then ultimately realize that we aren't. Living a strong spiritual life puts compassion, love, generosity, humility, and forgiveness highest on our list of priorities. We realize our limits and fallibility and have the security of knowing that God loves us no matter what; God will care for and protect us, support us, and encourage us when difficult situations arise.

The Bible helps us learn to rely on God. But God also relies on us to make a meaningful difference in the world. Parker Palmer, in *The Active Life*, says that "to be fully alive is to act. Through action we both express and learn something of who we are." People who develop a sense of purpose and meaning in their lives have a focus that keeps them moving forward. They are less likely to be distracted and upset by annoyances and the limitations of others.

Healing anger comes from widening one's focus and understanding how much pain and suffering exists in the world. From there, it is important to develop a purpose and take some type of meaningful action to make the world a better place. This can involve feeding the poor, helping with social causes, bringing food to the sick, building houses for the homeless, helping the lonely, the oppressed, the forgotten. There are so many things a person can do to make a worthwhile difference.

Some people are fortunate to be able to earn their living by doing something worthwhile for others. Other people use their spare time to help others, and they gain a sense of satisfaction and joy out of their volunteer work. Whichever it is for you, it is vital that you find some outlet for your energy, some cause to support, some worthwhile enterprise into which to put your time and effort.

You might believe you are already too busy to help anyone else. However, if you make the time to do something worthwhile for others, you will discover that you have more time than you thought. Your problems will not loom so large, and the things you tend to fret about will shrink by comparison. Bill works with AIDS patients, helping them get to doctors appointments. Jenny works with terminally ill patients in hospices, who are living out their last months of life. Both Bill and Jenny have noticed that their lives have changed drastically since they started their volunteer work. Bill says he no longer complains when it rains. Jenny is less irate about her mother-in-law's telephone calls. The things that used to bother them greatly are now no more than simple annoyances. Helping others moves the focus away from ourselves and helps people develop maturity and a sense of purpose. This, in turn, results in a new appreciation for what really matters in life. Small disappointments remain small and self-righteous anger decreases.

Are there some programs or projects that could use your help? Is there some organization that could benefit from a few of your hours? You will discover, as you offer your time to serve others, that you begin to feel a fullness as your spiritual hunger is fed. God will seem to be more present, and you will be more aware of your blessings. It is more difficult to maintain anger when you experience yourself as part of the larger picture, making a meaningful difference in your neighborhood or community. Your anger is redirected into speaking out or acting on someone else's behalf. In that way, self-centered anger is transformed into constructive, outer-directed, and justice-seeking energy.

Human beings are meaning-seeking creatures. We spend many years in school studying subjects but not necessarily figuring out who we are, what we are called to do, and how we fit this calling into the marketplace. When Todd, 20, came to me, his faculty adviser, he had little idea about what he wanted to do with his life. We devised a plan whereby he would discover his gifts and talents and try to see what career path might fit best for him. He first took an interest inventory, which gave a profile of his interests. He liked working with people and thus scored very high in that area. We then discussed what kinds of activities gave him a feeling of genuine pleasure and accomplishment. These were the activities that helped him feel most alive, most in touch with himself, and most purposeful. He made a list of these activities and also listed his particular talents—talking with people, being a good listener, having creative ideas. With his list of talents and a list of activities completed, we brainstormed different ways he could use his talents in career activities. He decided to wanted to go into the field of counseling, where he thought he would be effective as a family therapist.

When people have a sense of purpose, they have a greater sense of who they are and where they are going. They develop a larger picture of what is truly important to them and find the irritations and stresses of life less aggravating and difficult to handle than do those without a purpose. A small annoyance on the highway becomes just that—no big deal. As Todd learned more about himself and developed his personal mission statement, he gained a sense of confidence and peace. This directedness helped him put minor irritations in perspective and gave him hope for making a meaningful difference in the future.

Moving into Action

1. Make a list of your gifts and talents.

2. List the activities that you engage in that make you feel especially alive, most exuberant.

3. Write a personal mission statement. What is your mission in life? How will you carry it out?

7

GIVING ANGER A POSITIVE OUTLET

When you transform the enormous power anger makes available and apply it to the problems in your life, you suddenly realize you don't have to remain trapped by painful experiences. You can break free of the hold of a miserable set of hurtful and frustrating events. You can clear your life of resentment-causing problems. This makes it possible for you to freely pursue the important goals in your life.

— Neil Clark Warren, *Make Anger Your Ally*

WE HAVE LEARNED THAT OUR ANGER can be useful to us in many ways. It connects us with others. It tells us that we are alive. It signals that something may be wrong and we need to take action. Anger can motivate and stimulate us to seek justice, right wrongs, and make a difference. How do you use your anger to create a better world?

As mentioned in chapter 1, a group of women who were angry about the deaths of their children formed Mothers Against Drunk Driving (MADD). They decided that laws needed to be changed and that people needed to be made more aware of the devastation caused by those driving under the influence of alcohol. Members of this group speak all over the country about the hazards of drunk driving. They sponsor guest speakers who visit high school classes, and they have at times arranged for the wreckage of drunk driving accidents to be placed on the front lawns of schools as visual reminders of the danger. These women are good examples of people who turned their anger into something positive and necessary.

Similarly, after their son Jacob was kidnapped, the Wetterling family of Minnesota established the Jacob Wetterling Foundation. This foundation is designed to help other families deal with the agony they experience when a child is missing. It provides help and support for parents who are overwhelmed by this unexpected loss of a child. The Wetterlings have grieved. They were in denial for a long time, then angry, then sad, and then finally came to accept the loss of Jacob. Although they will never forget their son, they have steered their anger and grief into a positive organization.

My anger at being bullied and seeing the bullying that goes on in schools, on playgrounds, and on school buses resulted in my designing workshops around this issue and presenting it to parents all over the country. I turned my anger about violence, bullying, and domination issues into something constructive: a program for parents and educators and a book, *Raising Nonviolent Children in a Violent World.*

Other people have also chosen a lifework due to anger about a situation they encountered in their lives. Some educators of gifted children teach because they were frustrated and bored in school, angry that they were not challenged by their teachers. Some people go into mediation or collaborative law practices because they suffered through an adversarial divorce situation. Many parent educators decide to teach parents good disciplining skills because they were angry about the ways in which they were raised as children. Still others go into politics because they are angry about how the system ignores the plight of some of its disadvantaged citizens. Some of the work done for civil rights was the direct result of anger at the way black people were treated.

We live in a society that includes many angry people. Some of those who are angry feel oppressed, economically disadvantaged, and marginalized. We have a responsibility as children of God to try to create a more just society, and in this way we can heal the anger of oppressed groups. To do so, we have to put effort into promoting peace, equality, and opportunity for all. For some people, this means helping a group of low-income individuals start a business. It might mean creating housing for those who could not otherwise afford it, perhaps through such efforts as those undertaken by Habitat for Humanity.

We can't do everything, but we can each start somewhere. Pick a cause. Do something useful and helpful for someone in need. Educate people. Help create new laws that provide assistance and opportunities for marginalized people. Point out injustice wherever you see it. Boycott products that use ads to promote stereotypes. In actively fighting ageism, racism, sexism, and heterosexism, we hope to lessen the anger of those who are oppressed. Attend meetings and rallies. Sign petitions. Vote. But most of all, watch for the link between anger and oppression and realize that nobody is really safe until everybody is safe.

Moving into Action

1. Find something you believe in and fight for it. It may be building homes for the poor, conserving energy, or protecting wildlife. Take your anger about some injustice and put it to constructive use by supporting a cause you believe in. Join an organization that fights for rights for the oppressed. Talk to people in groups such as Mothers Against Drunk Driving about how they got started.

2. Learn about yourself by examining what makes you angry. Write in a journal about your anger to discover its roots. Find out how much of your anger is self-centered and how much of it grows out of a concern for other people. Be open to your potential to grow emotionally and spiritually as you do this.

3. Teach others how to manage and control their anger. Be a role model to help others, especially children, learn the difference between constructive and destructive anger.

4. Be an example of kindness, forgiveness, and acceptance. Once you become aware of your own anger, work on healing your destructive anger and allow your constructive anger to motivate you to a new level of personal and spiritual growth. Turn your anger into praying about what needs to be changed in our society.

5. Motivate others to help create a more just world by teaching them how to put their anger to constructive use.

CONCLUSION

There are times when anger is incorrectly associated with trivial matters. And there are times when it may be associated with legitimate concerns, but is managed irresponsibly. Balance is found when anger is linked to a reasonable issue and is communicated in a proper manner.

— Les Carter, and Frank Minirth
The Anger Workbook

WE LIVE IN DIFFICULT TIMES. Many people experience stress and frustration. Some of them become belligerent as a result. Violence and negativity often fill the news we watch, and there is much in our world that is beyond our control. Even the most trivial behaviors sometimes irritate and annoy people. Children kill children, and road ragers threaten and hurt innocent people on the streets and highways.

We have learned that anger can be our ally and can protect us, motivate us, inspire us, and connect us. We have also learned that many people's anger explodes into the destruction of others, and often of themselves.

As spiritually growing people, we can control our own angry moments through conscious choices. We can learn to manage our responses to situations and other people and discover longer-term healing methods that bring us closer to God, closer to others, and closer to a sense of peace and joy.

In order to heal our anger, we must connect spiritually with all of creation. We must become aware, from moment to moment, that God's grace and love abounds and is the answer to any difficulty, suffering, or disappointment. As we become more aware of God's presence and nurturing in our lives, we learn that we will receive everything that we need. This reassurance makes us less frantic, less angry, less in need to control everything and everyone around us.

If we surround ourselves with loving and supportive people, we will have the care and understanding that we need to help us cope with whatever life brings to us. Being grateful, patient, kind, humble, and forgiving, we will no longer need to let our self-righteous anger get the best of us.

We can also learn to use our anger to create a more just and caring world, and we can learn from our anger where our unique gifts might be. With purpose, persistence, and patience, we can help build a world that is more loving and compassionate.

> *Let everyone be quick to listen, slow to speak, slow to anger;*
> *for your anger does not produce God's righteousness.*
>
> — James 1:19-20

BIBLIOGRAPHY

Anger

Allicorn, Seth. *Anger in the Workplace: Understanding the Causes of Aggression and Violence.* Westport, Conn.: Quorum Books, 1994.

American Psychological Association (APA). *Controlling Anger before It Controls You* [WWW document], <http://helping.apa.org/daily/anger.html>, 1997.

Bach, George R. *The Inner Enemy: How to Fight Fair with Yourself.* New York: William Morrow, 1983.

Bushman, Brad J., Roy F. Baumeister, and Angela D. Stack. "Catharsis, Aggression, and Persuasive Influence: Self-Fulfilling or Self-Defeating Prophecies?" *Journal of Personality and Social Psychology* 76, no. 3 (January 1999): 367–76.

Campbell, Anne. *Men, Women, and Aggression.* New York: Basic Books, 1993.

Carter, Les and Frank Minirth. *The Anger Workbook.* Nashville: Thomas Nelson Publishers, 1993.

Decker, David. *Stopping the Violence: A Group Model to Change Men's Abusive Attitudes and Behaviors.* New York: Haworth Press, 1999.

Descimer, Jeane F. *The Killing Habit: Anger Control for Battering Couples.* New York: Free Press, 1984.

Doty, Betty. *Shake the Anger Habit.* Redding, Calif.: Bookery, 1990.

Freeman, Lucy. *Our Inner World of Rage: Understanding and Transforming the Power of Anger.* New York: Continuum, 1990.

Gaylin, Willard. *The Rage Within: Anger in Modern Life.* New York: Simon and Schuster, 1984.

Gelinas, Paul J. *Coping with Anger.* New York: Rosen Publishing Group, 1988.

Hankins, Gary. *Prescription for Anger: Coping with Angry Feelings and Angry People.* Beaverton, Oreg.: Princess Publishing, 1988.

Hough, Arthur. *Let's Have It Out: The Bare-Bones Manual of Fair Fighting.* Minneapolis: Compcare Publishers, 1991.

Johnston, Marianne. *Dealing with Anger.* New York: PowerKids Press, 1996.

Lee, John. *Feeling the Fire: Experiencing and Expressing Anger Appropriately.* New York: Bantam Books, 1993.

Leonard, Marcia. *Angry.* San Diego, Calif.: Smart Kids Publishing, 1997.

Lerner, Harriet. *Dance of Anger.* New York: Perennial Library, 1986.

Luhn, Rebecca. *Managing Anger: Methods for a Happier and Healthier Life.* Los Altos, Calif.: Crisp Publications, 1992.

McCafferty, Dennis. "Putting the Brakes on Road Rage." *USA Weekend.* 16 August 1998, p. 4.

McKay, Matthew. *When Anger Hurts: Quieting the Storm Within.* Oakland: New Harbinger Publications, 1989.

Nuckois, Cardwell C. *Healing an Angry Heart: Finding Solace in a Hostile World.* Deerfield Beach, Fla.: Health Communications, 1996.

Nye, Budd. *Understanding and Managing Your Anger and Aggression.* Federal Way, Wash.: BCA Publishing, 1993.

Potter-Efron, Ron. *Angry All the Time: An Emergency Guide to Anger Control.* Oakland: New Harbinger Publications, 1994.

_____. *Letting Go of Anger: The Ten Most Common Anger Styles and What to Do about Them.* Oakland: New Harbinger Publications, 1995.

Samalin, Nancy. *Love and Anger: The Parental Dilemma.* New York: Viking Press, 1991.

Sehnert, Keith W. *Dr. Sehnert's New Guide to Managing Your Stress.* Minneapolis: Augsburg Fortress, 1998.

Tavris, Carol. *Anger: The Misunderstood Emotion.* New York: Simon and Schuster, 1989.

Warren, Neil Clark. *Make Anger Your Ally.* Brentwood, Tenn.: Wolgemuth and Hyatt Publishers, 1990.

Williams, Redford and Virginia Williams. *Anger Kills: Seventeen Strategies for Controlling the Hostility That Can Harm Your Health.* New York: HarperCollins, 1993.

Forgiveness

Carter, Les and Frank Minirth. *The Choosing to Forgive Workbook.* Nashville: Thomas Nelson Publishers, 1997.
Simon, Sidney and Suzanne Simon. *Forgiveness.* New York: Warner Books, 1990.
Van Biema, David. "Should All Be Forgiven?" *Time* 153, no. 13 (5 April 1999).

Spirituality

Borysenko, Joan. *Minding the Body, Mending the Mind.* New York: Bantam Books, 1988, pp. 169, 170–71.
Nouwen, Henri J. M. *Life of the Beloved.* New York: Crossroad, 1992.
Palmer, Parker. *The Active Life.* San Francisco: Harper San Francisco, 1990, p. 17.
Puls, Joan. *A Spirituality of Compassion.* Mystic, Conn.: Twenty-Third Publications, 1988.
Smedes, Lewis B. *Shame and Grace.* San Francisco: Harper San Francisco, 1993, pp. 108, 164.
Veninga, Robert. *A Gift of Hope: How We Survive Our Tragedies.* Boston: Little, Brown, 1985.
Viorst, Judith. *Necessary Losses.* New York: Fawcett, 1987.

Personal Growth and Development

Dickinson, George E., and Michael R. Leming. *Understanding Families: Diversity, Continuity, and Change.* Fort Worth: Harcourt Brace College Publishers, 1995.
Gurian, Michael. *The Wonder of Boys.* Los Angeles: Tarcher, 1997.
Kübler-Ross, Elizabeth. *Death: A Final Stage of Growth.* New York: Simon and Schuster, 1997.
Obsatz, Michael. *Raising Nonviolent Children in a Violent World.* Minneapolis: Augsburg Fortress, 1998.
Pollock, William. *Real Boys.* New York: Random House, 1998.
Sheehy, Gail. *Understanding Men's Passages.* New York: Random House, 1998.

Storr, Anthony. *Solitude: A Return to Self.* New York: Ballantine Books, 1988.

Tannen, Deborah. *You Just Don't Understand.* New York: Ballantine Books, 1990.

Walsh, David. *Selling Out America's Children.* Minneapolis: Fairview Press, 1995.